HYSTERIA
A Collection of Madness

Stephanie M. Wytovich

RAW DOG
SCREAMING
PRESS

Previously published:
  Eclectic Flash Literary Magazine. "The Necklace." Print, 2010.
    § "The Necklace" was also included in their Best of 2010 Anthology. Jan. 2011.
  Niteblade Fantasy and Horror Magazine. "The Cheater." 2010.
  TDFS Publications. "Tell Me I'm Yours." 2010.
  Opium Magazine. "Signature." 2010.
  Whisper and Scream Magazine. "Bathtub Romance." 2010.
  Horror, Sleaze and Trash Magazine: "His First Time," and "Think of Me." 2010.
  Sex and Murder Magazine. "Unravel." 2010-11.
  Re-Vamp!. "Body Suit." 2011.
  Breadcrumb Scabs. "Lipstick." 2011.
  Night Train. "The Crematorium." 2011.
  The Horror Zine. "Chair Dance," and "On My Terms." 2011.
  Dark River Press: "Pick Up Line," and "Jumper." 2012.
  Horrotica Magazine. "Hysteria" and "Clean Break." 2013.
  The Wicked Library. "Winter," "Bathory," "Flower," and "Dead Roses."
    Audio, 2012-13.

Published by Raw Dog Screaming Press
Bowie, MD

First Edition

Cover illustration: Steven Archer
Book design: M. Garrow Bourke

ISBN 978-1-935738-49-7
LCCN 2013944332

Printed in the United States of America

www.RawDogScreaming.com

Contents

Dedication

This book is dedicated to the madness inside us all.
The madness we know is there, and the madness we don't.

Author's Note

I FIRST MET Hysteria a year ago. She came to me at night with madness in her eyes and pain etched in the corners of her cheeks. She wore a flowing, white dress stained with saliva and tears and when she spoke, I could hear her shake. Her lips were painted with dried blood and she rubbed her hands together like Lady Macbeth as if she'd already committed the crime without me.

Hysteria was a muse unlike any other that I've worked with, and she crept inside my mind like an ever-present nightmare that I couldn't get rid of. We spent insomnia-fueled nights together in the asylum as we explored the breaking points of the mind. We looked into the eyes of a killer, played inside the head of the deranged, and explored the psychosis of the truly insane. She held my hand as we walked down the wards and into the treatment rooms so she could shock me full of reality. Hysteria showed me the truth about people, and more importantly, she showed me what they were capable of.

Madness lives inside of us all.

It's just a matter of finding it, and knowing how to keep it hidden.

Stay Scared,
Stephanie M. Wytovich

The Muse Beneath the Madhouse

An Introduction to Hysteria

by Michael A. Arnzen

"HYSTERIA," AS YOU probably know, is a word we sometime use to describe raving madness. We go "hysterical" when we lose our minds and make a spectacle out of ourselves, excessively lashing out at the world. The term—which rose to popularity in psychoanalytic circles of the 19th Century psychoanalysis—might be common enough nowadays to be the title of a Def Leppard song, but psychology has abandoned the term, as it is something of a "catch-all" diagnosis that means everything and nothing—and more often than not has simply been a word that says "crazy" or "emotionally out of control." This wouldn't be a problem, if the word wasn't almost exclusively used in reference to women. "Hysteria" is a "women's disease"—a mental illness ostensibly originating "naturally" from a woman's body—in particular, the womb. It's been a word used to label women as crazy maybe when they've been guilty of being nothing more than women. And this may also have led many women with real, curable mental disorders over the past century or so to be misdiagnosed, or even worse, cured by the only "natural" method one would ultimately choose: throuh an unnecessary "hysterectomy."

I'm not here to write the history of this term, but if you want a good one check out Elaine Showalter's book, *Hystories*.

But do that later. For now, clutch the book you hold tightly and prepare to be horrified. The pages that follow have many sick and satanic surprises in store for you, but at the center of them all is Stephanie Wytovich's unblinking treatment of a woman's broken psyche. Her title is a sign of her overarching purpose: to reclaim the term "hysteria," and to use it as a way to explore a woman's madness through the lens of horror. She probably thinks it is simply a horror poetry book, but in it I see much more than that. In her introduction, we learn that "Hysteria" is the name Wytovich has given her dark muse. And what a nasty muse she is, for these pieces ask us to see through a madwoman's eyes quite often, with unthinkable results. And just as often, in page after page of this book we're attacked by the words and left to feel the sting in order to comprehend the depth of a woman's pain or a woman's desire that are often hidden or veiled by most representations of the feminine. I don't want to go so far as to say this is a "feminist" book, since it has higher ambitions than just being some kind of tract asking us to overthrow patriarchy. Instead, I'd like to think that it is more interested in madness itself. Wytovich is exploring gender reversals, and feminist ideas, but she's doing it in a way that may be just as skeptical of feminist claims as it is of anything else, as this is what the irrationality of madness can do: challenge our assumptions, sometimes by cutting right to the heart of the matter and extracting it before our very eyes.

Stephanie Wytovich embraces the tropes of the horror genre not just because she is a fan of its splatter films and psycho killers (which she is) but because she knows its history in the arts and sees the longstanding power of the irrational and unthinkable to challenge conventions. She understands that it is one of the most popular artforms to not be robbed of its aesthetic power by the mass market, because its emotional threats are also intellectual ones, giving the artist license to use the abnormal as a way to make us rethink what we assume to be normality. And her instincts are very good here, as this entire book—which is a healthy and meaty collection of poetry by a writer who is coming of age in the genre— delivers plenty of abnormal threats on every page.

Interestingly, the horror genre has been as male-dominated as the field of psychology over the past century, and in some ways has also been slowly evolving along with it. Wytovich is a part of that evolution, and while *Hysteria* is not necessarily a "feminist" book, per se, it brings a voice into the genre's conversation about identity in a way that I think is fantastic and very necessary. Stephanie Wytovich is working in a tradition of writers that run from Mary Shelley to Poppy Z. Brite—women who have refused to lobotomize the hysterical muse inside and instead have unleashed their dark side on the world. We really need to hear this voice more often.

So I'll shut up now and let "Wyto" speak for herself. I know she's waiting impatiently for you to come inside. I can hear her standing behind me, licking the razor. Hurry up and turn the page.

Mike Arnzen

8

A Killer Recipe

He didn't stand a chance
The ingredients were all there,
Mixed together and beat
With precision and love
And left to cook for 12 years

Alex wasn't born—
He was created,
Contrived meticulously
From the recipe his
Parents followed

When he was prepped
And aged to about 8 years,
They added a spoonful of physical abuse
Bought locally from dad's fists,
And added a dash of fire and gin,
Consumed daily underage
By the young boy's perverted mind

He sat for 2 years,
And they repeated until he broke

Then, dear Mom and Dad
Added a pinch of social awkwardness,
Picked fresh from the fields
Of a homegrown sociopath,
And blended them together
With the family's pet
That Alex
Recently slaughtered
In the outside shed

His rage was set to boil,
And they waited until
They saw a thick, red paste seep
Out the sides of his crust
Before they stuck in the pick
To see if he was done

His self pity was left to cool,
Until Alex's edges began to harden
Then during the final stage,
He was topped off with
A touch of the Oedipal Complex,
As sprinkles of hate and disgust
Were poured into his mouth

Alex was devoured by
Childhood taunts
And parental abandonment,
Until the timer went off,
And he snapped

Perhaps his parents
Should have read the
Warning label:
If tampered with,
Sour language and
A taste for sadism may occur
If so, rinse with regret
And repeat until guilt
Washes it away,
Or you're poisoned
From the consequences

Adulteress

Pray to God
When I find you
(and I will)
For there will be
No mercy shown
On my part

I intend
To show you
How it feels
To cry rivers
From so much
Pain,
To beg for
Death just to
Stop the hurt

I'll show you
How it feels
To have your
Heart ripped
Out and thrown
Away like trash
But it won't be
Your chest that
Meets my scalpel

No—
In fact,
Consider it
A blessing
When I sew your

Eyes shut
Because then you
Won't see what
I plan on doing
To her

This way,
You can just
Use your imagination
And listen to
How I can make
Her scream

Axed

Getting axed was the least of his worries
He was more concerned
With how his hair looked
Slicked back with blood
Than he was about it rolling around
On the ground like a soccer ball

Baby Bump

When they're pregnant—
Filled up with life,
Bursting with a motherly glow—
Is when I like to take them
Because I feel like I'm
Having a threesome—
Getting two for the price of one

Bathery

Her hair cascaded
    Down her back
In a flight of ravens
Against milk-white flesh
Bloodied from her
Midnight suitor

Drained of her age
She bathed in virginity
    Rubbing it into
Her skin to moisturize
The wear on her body
Collected from centuries past

Her fingernails
    Cut like knives
As she opened their chests
Shearing them like wool
So she could steal their years
To regain her youth

She drank their juices,
Savoring the crimson elixirs
    Each its own brand
Like a fresh, summer wine
Ripened in its adolescence
Begging to breathe

Her children sang
    Songs of death
Butchered at the hands
Of unattainable vanity

Courtesy of the Hungarian devil
Erzsebet, the countess of blood

Bathtub Romance

Water gushed over me
My lungs burned in its grasp
I couldn't breathe

Naked in flesh and spirit
I opened my eyes,
Took in the blurred world
Around me.

Pain elevated
I opened my mouth
Took my last drink.

Bind

I can't get off
Unless I'm
Strapped
Down,
Bound to the
Chair
And unable
To move,
Mouth taped
Stripped
Naked
And
Coughing
From your
Hands around
My neck

Bite the Bullet

I taste the gritty powder,
Wrap my tongue around
His thick barrel
And suck on his smooth shaft
The metal seduces my tastebuds
Entices me to push it further,
Slide it deeper down my throat
I can't deny the pleasure
Or how good it feels to choke
And I'm excited for the climax
When the bullet glides down my throat

Black Bird

I ask of you,
Can a dead soul cry?
Can it weep tears of blood
As it wails in the shadows
Of lost loves and empty bottles?
Can it mourn the memories
Of abandonment and neglect,
Sew up the prideful wounds
Of ink-spattered rejection,
Cast out in the dust-covered
Compositions no one got to read?

I ask of you,
Can a heart still hurt
After its stopped beating?
Does pain fade into the ether
Of dusk into dawn while
Ravens sing their funeral songs
Over his rose-laden grave?
Do they mock him in unison?
Squawking at the man who
Died for his art, whose words
Wove madness into a definition
Of sanity? Whose stories bled
Out like a Tell-Tale Heart,
Whose metaphors tapped
At our doors, relentlessly
Questioning our reason,
Our judgment, our sobriety?
Nevermore!

I ask of you,

Does the damned fear
The shape of death?
Does it cringe at the fluttering
Blackness that hangs over its head
Like a dark cloud in the blue sky?
Does the winged beast unsettle
Even the deadliest of creatures?
A marauder even to the master
That brought it to life? Does the
Raven speak blasphemy, rhyming
With a serpent's tongue, eyes gleaming,
Like a "demon that is dreaming?"
Can it see into our souls?

I ask of you,
Does the feather of the
Black bird bring the reaper?
Arms open, scythe extended,
No more questions,
Nevermore!

Blood Cocktails

Turning to her lover,
She asked for another drink
And like the gentleman he was,
He slit his wrist,
And brought it up to her
Scarlet lips

Blood Whiskey

His kiss tasted like whiskey
Soft coming in
Rough going down
And like an addict
I kept drinking
Trying to fill the void
The emptiness,
Anything to suppress
The thirst

His tongue danced
In my mouth,
Crept down my throat,
And I let it
Because it felt good,
Felt normal,
Like this was what
People were
Supposed to do,
Supposed to enjoy

But I wasn't normal
And I don't
Drink whiskey,
Never cared much
For the taste,
And as for the kiss,
Saliva wasn't what
I wanted to trade

I wanted his blood—
That crimson, bitter

Fluid that stains
My teeth red
And wets the
Area in between
My thighs

That velvety liquid
That lightens my flesh
Bringing youth
To my once weary eyes,
Taking away my years
Replacing them
With his

Yes
I wanted his life
So I took it,
And before the night
Was over,
I was drunk
On his death

Body Suit

Unzip my spine
I'm suffocating in here;
Layer upon layer of
Skin and muscles
Sweltering in the heat
Frying in the air—
This flesh suit is too hot,
Boiling my sweat as it
Steams out my pores—
Blistering my beige jacket
Melting off my Gucci buttons
Leaving my khaki pants
Stuck to my bones

I'm wondering when
These air bags I call lungs
Are going to explode
From the pressure—
Releasing the built up tension
Of cancerous poisons that
Have been pumped into me
Year after year, eating away
The ashes of my organs,
Turning my cells against each other—
Cannibals of red on red, white on white
Engulfing both body and spirit

I ache to feel the breeze
Against my vertebrae,
To listen to the whistle
Of the wind between my clavicle
And touch the draft gliding

Across my breastbone
So it's time to leave behind
This old carcass jumper
Step out into the real world
With my shiny new attitude,
Fresh off the press smell,
And skeletal grip on life

Bracelet of Blades

Sifted through
Bathroom cabinets
Look disheveled
As they hang in a mess of
Scattered cotton balls and
Spilled Iodine
Sitting amongst half-full
Pill boxes and
Empty bottles of Nyquil

Sweat-stained towels
Litter the cracked
Linoleum floor,
And when she dropped
To her knees,
Her skin stuck
To the hair-sprayed
Tiles like
A bathing suit
Suctioned to wet flesh

Starving for pain,
For her mental release,
She snapped off
The plastic holders
Of her razors
And shook out their blades,
Repeating the process
Over
And
Over
Like a child learning

A new game

She sat there
Surrounded by old friends,
As she started to weave
Them in and out
Of her wrists,
Wearing them like a
New, metallic bracelet
Adorned in crimson red

Braided

I cut off a lock of your hair
When you slept last night.
I don't think you'll be able to tell,
But I want you to know that I've
Taken really good care of it.
I even braided it before I tucked
It into the front pocket of my jeans
This morning.

Sometimes during the day,
When I can't take it anymore
And I just miss you so much,
I'll slip it out and smell it,
Run it across my upper lip
And take in the perfumed smell
Of your shampoo.
The lavender scent calms me down
And the soft hint of chamomile
Really helps with the urges,
So thank you for that!

Really,
I think it's quite romantic.
Guys used to do this
In the old days, you know?
Keep a lock of their lady's hair
With them so they could take
It out and fondle it,
Induce fantasies and pass the
Time until they saw their
Lovers again.

I hope you're not mad,
But it's hard when I can't
See you all the time, and
You haven't returned my
Phone calls in ages,
So I figured a memento
Would have to suffice
Until you finally came around;
And don't worry,
I know you didn't mean it
When you had the cops
Take me away the other night—
It was just a misunderstanding.
But you'll see me soon,
So until then,
Think of me when you
Wash your hair this morning
And do us both a favor—
Wear it down for tonight.

Burnt Hair

If Elvis could
Die on the toilet
And still be famous,
I figured I didn't
Need a sad Kurt Cobain
Death where people
Speculated murder
And pointed fingers
At sloppy blondes—
All I needed was
A spark and a decent
Head shot with glassed over eyes
To finish off my portfolio

I thought about
Going out with a bang!
But guns are so last season,
Yet pills seem too obvious
Of a choice for a starving
Cover girl like myself,
And I've gone under the knife
Too many times for anyone
To appreciate
That sharp mess of irony

I looked at my options,
Maybe a one-step
Two–step hustle
Off the roof,
Or a run-in with a
Jealous ex gone wrong
But they'd all been

Done before
Even though the tabloids
All say that killing
Never goes out of style,
That suicide is the
Next big thing
But originality…
That's the secret
To infamy
And I was already
Known for my hair

The choice seemed
Obvious in the end,
After I dyed and
Straightened my curls,
I stood in the shower
With my hair dryer
And turned the water on

The fucking sparks
Ruined my follicles,
Fried my ends,
Made them frizzy
As a lion's mane—
I looked like a
Drowned rat in
Lacy Lingerie
As I dropped in the tub
And sat in what looked
Like shit-stained water
From the auburn color
I used on my roots

Worst yet,
In the paparazzi

Money-shot
My eyes were closed
And after two days,
The hype died down—
No one even remembered
The girl that killed herself
To get a flicker of fame

Chair Dance

It was a race to the top—
A sprint for a chair that
Would end up being
Toppled over anyways,
And I prayed for once
In my life, that I would not
Finish second best to you,
That I would get there
First this time,
So you couldn't take away
The spotlight from me
When I danced
In front of the family
Tomorrow morning

Choke Me

Eight fingers tie around my neck
Two thumbs pressed together
At the middle,
They form a 'W'
For win

Clean Break

Cracked bones
Splinter
Through open
Flesh
Like a corpse
Clawing
Out of its
Grave
Leading the
Way for
Others
That dig at her
Skin,
Tear at it,
Scraping
Like animals
Looking
For food
Until
There's
Nothing left
But
Pale sticks
Poking
Out her leg
Signaling
For the
Rest to follow

Comatose

I'm awake, but the night,
Like an abusive ex, cannot let me go.
It does not know how to live
Without the pulsating sight
Of my veins against the shadows.
The echoes of my screams
Trapped under mounds of blankets
Or the suffocating stench
Of fresh urine on tear-stained sheets

Without me filling its void,
It would have no female to birth the
Murderous reflections of hospital mirrors—
The steel-rimmed ovals that harbor attempted suicides
And the profiles of mental patients drunk on death

Its growth could not penetrate nightmares,
Could not fuck the darkness any deeper
Into my head, letting demons run loose
In an imagination fueled by sadism

My thighs bleed black against the white hospital gown,
A Rorschach test born out of agony
And broken claws that feel like nails
Midnight feeds off my misery
Eats away at pieces of charred flesh
From the cigarette burns in my arms,
It allows darkness to drink from the slits in my wrists
Draining me, but never to the point of death
Because without me, Night would be alone
Left in solitary where it belongs,
But like a fool, the doctors don't realize

That bars won't keep him in,
That he can slide out like smoke
And continue to rape me every night

Compulsions

One.
Two.
Tap, tap
Wipe hands
On pants
Three.
Four.
Tap tap tap
Flip light switch
On, off.
On, off.
On.
Five.
Six.
Tap tap
Wash hands,
Dry till raw
Scrub, scrub scrub
Seven.
Eight.
Tap Tap Tap
Did I turn the
Light off?
Nine.
Ten.
Start over
Again.

Con Artist

Every Tuesday
I come here
Religiously
To keep tabs
On you and
Make sure I'm
Still on target

I sit in the red
Comfy chair off
To the right,
People-watching
In the café,
Trying to pick up
Pieces of my neighbors'
Conversations
While I copy their
Mannerisms
And commit them
To memory

Sometimes
I've found that
If I concentrate
Hard enough
I can copy an accent,
Or mimic a
Speech impediment
And perfect the way,
That the girl, to my left,
The one who orders
A spiced vanilla latte,

Every day at
2 o'clock,
Speaks with a lisp

But you,
Well…
You've gotten
Predictable
And I'm starting to
Lose interest
Like a man who
Has been screwing
The same whore
Every night for the
Past week

But repetition is
Good.
Repetition is
Safe.
It's what keeps
Men like me
In business
And food
On the table

So I'll ride you
A little longer,
And watch as
You push that strand
Of hair behind
Your ear…
Giggling while you
Sip your espresso and
Try to pretend that
You don't recognize the

Guy in the corner,
The one near the fireplace
That's fucking you
With his eyes

But then again,
You're not the most
Observant person
I've ever stalked,
I mean
Hell,
You don't notice me
Either
And I've been
Stealing your identity
For over
Two months now

Confession

Everyone's favorite question to ask me is why.
Why did I do it?
Why would I do something to destroy so many innocent lives?
Something so horrible, that it takes
The threat of death to get me to confess?
Why do I write down such terrible things?
Put people in such horrid situations?
Drown them. Torture them.
Murder them.
Well, why is a big question—
It's philosophical.
Spiritual.
Existential.
But mostly, it's bullshit.
Sometimes there is no reason.
Sometimes, they deserve it.
Most of the time they don't.
Sometimes, I just like to hear them scream.

Craving

His eyes were black
Two dark circles that
Looked like olives
Rolling around up there
Waiting to be plucked out
And thrown on a plate
I stared at them
With a wet palate
And popped them out
With the switchblade
In my pocket
For I had missed dinner
And was craving something Greek

Crazy

Crazy is a term
For the weak,
For the living that can't
Finalize the death they
See on a daily basis,
That refuse to look at
The undead zombies
That walk the halls of this ward,
That breathe in the decrepit
Stench of the almost-corpses
That can't leave their beds,
And wouldn't if they could

Crazy is a term
For the unwilling,
For the patients that continue
To take their medication,
Believing that the pills
Will help them,
Will make them better,
When they're only prolonging
The inevitable blackness
That will consume them,
And strangle them from
The inside out

Crazy is what they call me,
But I'm only crazy
Because I'm sane!
Because I see the reaper
Standing in the corner of my room,
Waving his scythe at me,

Saying hello
As he motions me forward
And I don't deny him
The soul he so rightfully
Deserves to claim

I offer myself,
The tragedy of what
I learned to call my life,
Into his ether-cloaked arms
And accept death as he
Stands before me,
Acknowledging him as my father
As we walk hand and hand
Down the hallway,
But they won't let me leave,
And they won't let me die
So despite my acceptance
Of the black marauder
That beckons me in my sleep,
I cannot go to him
Because my sanity
Grounds me in this hospital
In this room,
To mingle among the undead souls
That poke and prod me
Slowly turning me mad

Crazy Eights

It's something about their hair,
Their coarse, wiry follicles
And the way they get lodged
In my throat
Like fury splinters
Stuck to the sides of my esophagus
That makes me smile

I typically pluck out their eyes,
Munch on them
Like miniature chocolates
Suck out their juice
To recycle their blood
And use their legs
As toothpicks,
Savoring their hisses
As I rip the limbs off
Their plump, rounded bodies

The venom adds an exotic taste
When you milk it from
Their fangs,
I like to add it in
With my morning coffee,
Right after I feed my pets
That way in a few hours
They will be fat and full
And ready for my lunch

Darkness

It gets dark in here
When they shut the door
They like to think
It scares me
But I feel safer when
The jackets lock me up
And kidnap the light

It's comforting
Knowing that I'm
Alone in here with
No one to harm me
But myself—
No guarantees of course,
Although ideas
Tend to be harmless
Unless you act on them

Yet if I've learned anything
In my time here,
It's that it's ok to hear the voices—
You just don't want to
Start answering them back

Dead Roses

I keep a dead rose on my desk
To remind me that everything
Beautiful eventually has to die,
That life has a way of subtracting
Even when it all seems perfect

I keep a dead rose on my desk
To remember that hearts can break,
And not be put back together again,
That pain doesn't fall off slow
Like crisp, wilted petals
But rather hits the body hard
With the strength of a thousand thorns

I keep a dead rose on my desk
To prove that I can face you,
That your memory doesn't haunt me
Like the smell of smoke and metal,
That the crimson color of my décor
Doesn't remind me of your blood

Doctor's Orders

They can't retaliate,
Their lives depend on me!
Me, with my prescription pad,
A pill box full of hope

I own them all
My personal family of headcases
That fuel my urges,
Stand in for my experiments
Say and do what I tell them
Out of fear from the voices
In their heads

It's funny what a person
Will do when you take
Away their chance at sanity,
Remove their small ounce of happiness

The women will spread their legs,
The men bow their heads in your lap
All for a pill that grants
Momentary serenity,
A placebo that they think
Will help them
But just gets me off

Drummer Boy

Poison runs through my head
Like rivers coursing downstream
Passing over the rocks of my past
Collecting in the oceans
Of memories yet to come

The liquid burns,
Fills my skull with drums
That never cease to stop
They pound, pound, pound,
Ringing through my ears
I beg for them to quit,
To just give me a second
Of silence, of peace,
But they bang louder
As the nurses fill me up
Adding more juice
To an already full container

I fear that I'll spring a leak,
That my head won't be able to
Hold it all,
That my brain will
Drain out from my orifices and
Leave a puddle on the floor
That they'll end up feeding me,
Stuffing me full of myself
Through a tube,
I'll be a cannibal
Flesh of my flesh,
Blood of my blood
I'll silence this drumming
By eating the drums

Energy Surge

He likes me
Because I'm quiet,
Not because he knows
I'm eating his spirits
As he walks on by

But I'm silent and fast
For his soul tastes bitter,
Even though his energy is sweet—
A sugary treat for a man
That feeds on auras
To drain that bastard's
Vigor and keep him at bay

You see,
He thinks he has me,
Thinks he has me wrapped
Around his finger
As he feeds me meds
And visits me at night,
But each time he enters me,
Each time he takes me
Without my permission,
He dies a little more
And a little faster

Eye Appointment

The doctor held
A black patch
On a wooden stick
Up to my right eye,
Asked me to concentrate,
Tell her what
Letter I saw

"Six," I said.

Confusion stormed
Her store-bought face
As she switched over
To my left
Hoping for better results

"Six," I said.

She yelled at me,
Told me she didn't
Think this was funny,
Told me to read the
Board as it was
And stop playing
Games

"Six," I said.

She threw down
Her instrument,
Screamed something
About not getting paid

Enough for this shit,
Asked me if I knew
How to read

"Yes," I said.
"Can't you?
The board clearly states
You're going to die"

Fetish

I opened up the window,
Let the cool breeze caress my face
While I stuffed the rag in my mouth
And bit down hard

The floor was cold
But the razor was hot,
Burning red from laying in the flame
Sanitizing itself and prepping for its chore

My hands always shook before
The first incision, but
When I cut through my flesh,
I breathed a sigh of relief as I
Tediously drew etchings on my thighs,
Watching the red seep into view
As I hurriedly connected the dots

But it wasn't the pain that took away the hurt
The real elixir lay in my blood,
And when my tongue ran across my arm,
Lapping up the cherry gloss that slid across my wrists
I felt myself let go,
Relaxing with the taste of blood on my lips

Flower

Tulips—
Two lips pressed
Against each other
In harmony

Only to be replaced
By blood.
A pain that drips

Rubies on a
White, cotton dress.
A wedding dress

Ripped apart by
Moths in the attic,
Eaten away

At the throat
Where my pearl
Necklace used to

Hang. I sway
In the rafters,
Dancing shadows

On the walls
Where I know he'll
Find me.

He'll miss me
Someday. They
Always come looking.

Give Him the Floor

I watched as he
Screamed in his bed,
Ankles shackled with
Rubber bracelets,
Arms tied behind his head
Belting out a deafening
Shriek as if he were falling
Down the rabbit hole with Alice,
Being beaten by the floating objects
She so easily averted

His legs looked like rigid boards
Lifted off the cotton sheets,
Bones stiff, tight—
Like if they touched the mattress
They'd be burned from the
Imminent Hell that waited
For him in between the covers

And his eyes,
Those eyes!
They were bloodshot,
Bulging out of his skull like
Imagined flames licked at his ass,
Climbed up his anus like ants
Scurrying to food.
He shook from tension,
Veins pulsing as he tried
To hold himself
Above the bed turned grave,
His body jackhammering in fear
As I fed him

Muscle relaxers with needles
So he would calm down,
Lay down,
And embrace his fear

Glutton

He eats to feel full
But remains empty
After every bite,
Each delectable morsel
Disintegrating
Into cells of fat,
Sticking to the lard
That has become his shell
As he remains hollow

Greed

It overpowered me,
Tackled me at the legs
Took me down to the ground
Shoved the blood-soiled dirt
In my mouth

I tried to fight it,
Tried to shake the
Mental fuck job it did
To my head,
But I was consumed,
Too far gone to turn back
From the shadows
That overpowered me,
That grabbed me by the throat
And showed me the way

I took what I wanted
Fed when I pleased
Slept when I needed it
Obeyed no one but myself,
Listened, to none other
Than my own cravings
That pushed me in the direction
Of my deepest desires,
My most sought after lusts

I gave in to the black hole
That bled throughout my chest,
Worshiped at it
Like the peasant I was,
A mere nothing in the realms

Of earthly pleasures,
And for my servitude
I was awarded,
I was given gratification
For my sins,
Given eternal life
For my greed

Guardian Angel

They spread my arms and legs
Out like a four-pointed star,
Tightened my leather straps
And locked me in
Like some muskrat caught
Misbehavin' on their property,
They left me to die
While I continued prayin'
That I would
Prayin' to Jesus that
They'd get me off this ward,
Lock me up somewhere else

You say the wrong thing
Around here,
People start to think
You're crazy
Like madness is
Some contagion you
Breathe in through the air
I just told them that sweet
Jezebelle didn't like it
When the men talked
To her like that,
When they visited her
In her cell and touched
Her pretty face.
Ran their fingers
Through her silky hair

They beat me
To get out my crazy,

Fed me successions
Of multi-colored pills,
Clothed me in a hug-me jacket
With a matching skull cap
Wired to my head
Accessorized with
Stitches of electrodes

They shocked me full of pain
Left me naked in my cell—
Sweet Jezebelle didn't like that
Didn't like what those
White jackets did to me
With their devil-like grins
And their manhood stretchin'
To the top of their belts

She paid them a visit
Afterhours one night,
Stabbed 'em in the throat
With the sharpened edge
Of one of my buckles
Stickin' up for me like
Guardian angels always do
Puttin' those prison guards
In their rightful place,
Cold and bleedin' out
All over my black Mary Janes

Hallucination

Yes or no?
Are you there or not?
I can't hear you
The voices won't
Shut up

You're blurry—
A spinning
Splurge of colors
And it's hard to
Put a picture
To your face
When you're
Constantly in
Movement

Please
Slow down

I want to touch you
But you're far away
Even though
Your breath
Caresses the
Nape of neck
I cringe
Not knowing
Who you are
Even though
You're with me
Every day

Please
I'm begging you

Show yourself
Be with me
Decide I'm worth it
I don't know
How much longer
I can last

My mind—
It wanders
For you
And I'm afraid
It will get lost
If it keeps looking,
Keeps searching,
Delving deeper
Into this portal
Of madness
To which you
Hold me in

Hanging

Ol' Red was a fighter,
A prison junkie
With a reputation
That spurted blood
Like the arteries he stabbed
And the throats he slit

He'd spend his days
Locked away in his cell,
Starving till the point of madness,
So that when he came out
He'd be at the top of his game,
No challenger unworthy
Of the hands he'd turned
Into weapons
Or the rage he'd grown
Over the years in the hole

Ol' Red liked to fight dirty,
Hid shanks in his pockets
Forks in the belt loops of his pants,
And he'd sooner kill you
Just because you were alive
Than because you did
Something to piss him off

Even the chair couldn't beat him,
Couldn't spark his brain
Enough to put him down
So they tied a noose
Around a neck
And called all his friends

To come and watch him
Kick on stage

Head Banging

I don't see a reflection
When I look in the mirror
Because I see your face
An image that I can't part with
That won't leave me alone
Because you,
You're staring at me
Everywhere I look
As constant reminder of what I did

Those blue eyes of yours,
They're in everyone now
And I can see you in crowds of people
Plain as the day I carved up your face
Walking around with that sewn in smile
Limping from your broken left leg
Constantly there
All the time
Never letting me forget
Preventing me from moving on

Because you

You're fucking with my mind
Setting your necklace on fire
While it hangs around my neck,
Searing my skin with your initials
Burning your pain into me
While I hear your laugh in the basement
Like a cackle in the wind
That one that stops me in my steps
Making me envision your corpse

Standing at the foot of my bed

But you're dead!
You're dead!
So damn it, why won't you die!
Why can't you stay with your body
Buried in the ditch in the backyard
Gagged so I can't hear you scream
Eyes shut so I don't have to look in them
Eight feet underneath
Where you belong
Where you should be

But no
You're screwing with me, princess
But I watched you die and
I heard you scream
I know you're not real
I know you're not here
So get out of my head
Get out of my head
Out of my head

No
No

Then I'll force you out,
Just like I forced myself into you
I'll cut you out of me
Just like I cut out those pretty little blue eyes
Because if I'm gone, then you can't hurt me
No, you can't torment me
If I'm no longer here
Can you?
No.
And I can't hear you laughing anymore

With the barrel in my mouth
I can't taste your cherry lip gloss now,
Just metal against my teeth
And my reflection,
I'm in it now, not you
And pretty soon
My blood is going to be on that mirror,
Not yours
Not anymore
Just mine
Just mine
So get ready to swallow
Because this time
It won't be my cock in your mouth
Just a bullet that tastes like my kiss
One that gets rid of both of us
And let me tell you something, Princess
There are some things that are far worse than death
And if you thought I was bad as a mortal,
Just wait until I'm undead

His First Time

Close your eyes for a minute
Count to ten
Remember to breathe, dammit!
You're so pale
Did you think this was going to be easy?
It's your first time for Christ's sake!
Of course you're going to be nervous!

Calm down
Please just calm down,
What did you think was going to happen?
Fuck! Of course she is going to scream!
Wouldn't you if someone touched you like that?

Easy now,
EASY! You can't go that fast!
If you continue at that speed,
It will be over before it you know it.
Learn to savor it, child.
Enjoy the moment,
The pleasure

That's right
Touch her there
Move her hair out of her eyes,
So you can see that pretty lil face.
Now tell her to open that beautiful mouth of hers.
Jesus, child! Don't ask her to do it.
She only has one purpose
And that's to obey you

Nice, now put the gun in her mouth.

Oh stop your shaking… it's not so bad!
See the way her eyes are glistenin'?
She likes it child,
She wants more

Now tell her what you want her to do,
And how you want her to do it.
Girls like this will do anything son,
They just need some persuadin'

Go ahead now,
You do what you want child,
Mama will be inside,
But I'll leave the door open a lil
Just in case you need me
Plus, I like to hear the bitches scream, too

Hysteria

The Doctor
Called me crazy
Emotionally unstable
Led me into a fainting room
Sat me down
And took off my clothes
Hysteria, he called it
Treatable,
Yet dangerous
Common in women
Suffering from
Sexual deprivation
A sickness that if not
Attended to,
Would eventually kill me
You're diseased, he said
But I can cure you
If you let me
He turned the lights off
Shoved
A vibrator up my cunt
And told me to
Calm down,
Told me to relax and
Let go
But sex doesn't cure
Being a woman
When madness is
Bred into our blood
Courtesy of the bastards
That created us
Sex doesn't cure

Insanity,
Only God can do that

Imaginary Friend

There are monsters under my bed
Creatures in my head
They whisper things about you
Tell me stories about the dead

Their voices help me sleep
Watch me while I dream
They hug me while I shake
Black out my muted scream

The blankets don't protect me
Their threads just come undone
Nothing can try to hide me
Once they decided to come

Clawed hands reach up to get me
But I don't try to fight
These monsters are my friends
My playmates of the night

Incubus

The needle is full of juice
My arm bare and ready
I clench my hand into a fist,
But I don't want to go to sleep,
Don't want to see him again

The point enters my skin
Fills me full of fluid,
A white sap that knocks me out
Leaves me to wander
In a gray cloud of agony

I scream silence
And he breeds

His fingers move though
My hair like snakes,
His tongue weaves paths
Of saliva inside my mouth,
I cringe but he pulls my hair
Drags me deeper into the nightmare
And locks the door to my head

Insomnia

I've checked out into blackness,
Signed the waiver
For eternal consciousness
Accepted the red eyes
The bags built into my skin
And the ever present yawn
That's etched into the
Corners of my mouth

I've watched the sun come up,
Felt the burn in my corneas
From the rays of dawn,
And I've swam in the darkness
While I've wept at the moon,
Consuming its milk-white poison
Choking on exhaustion
But never dying

I left my punch card in the stars,
Now an ever present absentee
With no sense of time,
Just a floating anomaly in a sea of people
Who have the ability to pause,
To hit the red button and stop,
Who can close their eyes
And shut off the nightmares
While I suffer on rewind
In a cycle of repetition

Interrogation Room

He shined the
Light in my face
Say you're sorry
No
I said say it
I won't
He leaned over
The table,
Looked me right
In the eye,
Inches from my face,
And why not?
Because I liked it

Juliet

The Capulet wench
Drank poison to still her heart
When Romeo should
Have just reached in and removed it
As a trophy for the Monatgue's
For seducing a stupid girl
Into the hands of death

Jumper

Stop the ground
My wings aren't working
This is a mistake
And no one said it would hurt to fall
But the wind is chapping my lips
Stinging my eyes
And the concrete didn't cushion my face
Like you said it would

La Fee Verte

The more you drink
The more real she becomes;
A toxic vision in green,
Who will spread her wings
For those willing to stay
In their drink
And tempt fate
To see the sex-crazed glint
In her emerald eyes

But be warned,
She's a clever seductress;
Sweet like the sugar cube
You set on fire,
Yet lethal like the poison
You keep sliding
Down your throat

Lazy Eye

One stares straight ahead
The other wanders
Ever searching
For the bastard
That stabbed
And sheared it
From its path
Of normalcy

Legion

Men in purple ribbon
Throw water on
My face
Burn my skin
With their lies—
Their faith—
But I have her,
Wrapped
Up in her own
Limbs,
Tightly packaged
With my
Signature
Etched in her
Skin,
An inverted cross
Pointing her
Straight to me
And
No God
Of theirs
Can save her
Now

Lipstick

Since I was thirteen,
I wanted full, pouty lips
So I could gloss them up
And make a statement
In the crowd—

So every night,
I would prick myself
With my mother's
Sewing needle—ten times
On the lower lip—five
On the upper,
Barely sleeping through
The night because
I anticipated the outcome
With such excitement—
Such ardor, that I could
Finally look like the popular
Girls in homeroom—

And when I woke up
And saw the swollen flesh,
Bubbling with infection…
I couldn't help but smile

Lithium

Locked inside my head
I Ping-Pong back and forth
    Twitching in mania
        Drowning in depression
The back and forth act
Becomes too much
For an unbalanced junkie
Like my two-faced self
    I cry into bed sheets
        Laugh in my white-walled cell
No one comes to save me,
To tell me it's going to be ok
That they're just mood swings—
I'll probably grow out of them
    Half of me laughs
    The other half cries

Luna

They walked the woods
Tore down trees
Used them as toothpicks,
Spat out the splinters
And barked at the wind

I watched them at night,
Waltzing under stars
Like it was their birthright
To kill and feed on us
As if we were nothing more
Than meat sacks,
Walking bags of blood

The jackets found me naked,
Half-dead with slit wrists
Faded eyes blinded
From chains of silver

My hair was tussled
Woven with twigs
Strung up and braided
With fallen leaves,
I howled when they took me
Bit at them
When they locked me up
And turned off the moon

They called me wolf girl
But my name was Luna,
Named after the Goddess
Who made me what I am

Not what they think I am,
Sick, deranged,
A patient with a fetish
An obsession with the night sky
And the circle that hangs
Within it

Marketplace

I walked through the
Grocery store
Eyes glued to
Stainless steel hooks
That waved at me
In the butcher shop
Window
While I picked out
The freshest of meats

I knew little Janey
Liked the thick ones
Rare, with
Lots of fat
She said the extra tire
Around their waists
Gave them more flavor,
Added a little something
To the juice
When she tongued
It off her chin

So I brought her
Home a big one,
Chopped it up,
Sautéed it with
Green onions,
And let it soak in
Its own blood while it
Salted itself
And stewed in the pan

The smell of it
Brought her running,
Brought her
Scrambling down
The stairs,
Her stomach
Growling like the
Beast that baked
In the oven
Mommy! Mommy!
What's for dinner?
She asked
I scooped her out a
Helping of thigh
And served it warm
On her plate
Why it's Old man Donnell sweetie,
I know you've had
Your eyes on him
For quite a while

Masochist

He agitates my heart,
Sends me words that stick
Like hooks in my ears
But the pain—
    It's the pain
That made me sell
It in the first place,
Made me beg
For the torture,
Plead for the insanity,
    But I took it.
I took the bait just
Like a fish that nibbles
On maggots—
Those white, ghost worms
That now fester in my chest
Feeding on my
    Soulless corpse
I have no one to blame—
A slave to masochism
I bathe in the blood
Of my trade,
I was Lillith reborn in a cell
A blood countess
In the ways of virginity
    I ate the dreams
Of my ward mates
Like a succubus at night
So I could feel their agony
Breathe in the stench of suffering
All for the love of a shadow,
For the heart of the Reaper
Who held on to my soul

Memory Loss

The crevices
Carved in my mind
Drain sludge into my brain,
Drowning my memories,
Erasing my thoughts
Like Sunday School detention
I shake my head in hopes
That the liquid will run
Out my ear
But nothing, no elixir,
No poison seeps through
The orifices of the piñata
I call my head,
The stump that shakes
Like a rattle on this fragile neck,
Trying to remember what
It is that I'm doing here,
But the medicine fogs
Out my thoughts and each
Time I get closer
To figuring it out,
The bit is stuffed in my mouth
And the electrodes are
Strapped to my temples
One shock, two shock
Red shock, blue shock,
I ache for my childhood
For the recollection of my college years
But the electricity fries out
The months studying Byron
Reducing me to the crazed images
Of Thing 1 and Thing 2,
My hair now standing straight

Like a balloon has been rubbed
Through it and peppered with static
My words no better than
The Cat in the Hat,
My memory now reduced
To nothing more than a talking
Fish and a plate of *Green Eggs and Ham*
They expunged the person that I am
For the person that I was,
An adult who acts like a child
Rather than one who sleeps with them

Migraine

I fall deeper into this hole
Banging my head
Slicing my legs
Succumbing to the darkness
Dropping in blackness

The longer I plunge
The more I hold my breath
Just waiting for the razor blades
To stop cutting into my brain
To just bleed out
And go to sleep

But the drums keep playing
The blood keeps dripping
Slowly,
    Eating
Away at me
Digging its teeth
Into my transmitters
Telling me to end it
That death would be
More suitable

I claw at my hair
Ripping strands out
My fingers stained
With dye,
Crooked with pain
Tearing at flesh
To stop the beating
Stop the pounding
Kill the drummer

Mirror Talk

This face is not my own
>*Who am I?*

I don't know who is
Looking back at me
>*A ghost?*
>*A Survivor?*

There are hollow eyes—
Dead eyes—
That pierce me like needles,
Poke holes in my chest to
Make sure that I bleed
>*I do*

I remain alive
Despite the blood pooling
Around my feet
>*It sticks to me*
>*Like flesh*

The sallow sink of my cheeks,
Wrap around bone
My body folds in on itself
>*A yellow glow*
>*A pale reflection*

I'm covered in disease—
I'll wear this hospital gown
To my death

Moon Goddess

The moon does not see
The tears that weep
In this wooden box—
Does not hear the subtle
Drip of tears against
Splinters and sharpened stakes—
She merely hides her face
In the overcast
Blanketing her eyes
With the blue-gray clouds
Drinking in their moisture
Like fresh dew on a summer's eve

The goddess does not mourn,
Does not sadden over
A loss of one of her own,
She merely moves on,
Dancing through the galaxies
While I fester with the worms
That I wear on my neck like pearls

I call to sing my rehearsed moans
My howls that once sung 'Mother'
Unto her presence,
But she does not come back
Does not dig through the Earth
For her child,
Like a true daughter of the Gods,
She proceeds with an assumed
Grace, leaving the weak behind
Family or not,
To procreate a stronger line

That will birth children
Among the shadows to bow
And worship at her

Necro-let-me-feel-ya

My stomach is in a lover's knot
Twisted in desperation
As I gnaw on your insides
I miss the taste of your blue kiss
But your blood might be better
Because it gets me there quicker

I'll be your prisoner
If you be my crime-scene victim
Wrapped in yellow caution tape
As your dead eyes scream 'No!'
I'll even wear the police uniform
And cuff you to the guard rail,
Turn the lights on, red, white, blue
A private party for the opening act

You know I like it best
When you're cold and dirty,
When I have to wipe off the gravel,
Scrape the dirt from underneath your nails,
Adjust your stiff, rigid limbs
So I can enter you in the grave

There's no safe word when you're dead
Just the hard silence
That your icy lips can't speak against
And when I take you in the moonlight
I can scream knowing that you can't

No Vacancy

I can't afford another
Tenant
There's no room left
In my head
No space open
To lease out to little girls
With big screams
And big tits
But no matter how much
I want to let them in
They can never pay the rent,
So they end up
Staying with me
Their faces locked
In my head,
Their bodies buried
Underneath my
Floor boards

Nurse in Ward # 1

I like it when it rains
Because the air
Has a reason to feel cold,
And I'm not constantly
Reminded that there are
People around me
Moments from death,
Practically knocking down
The Reaper's door
To escape

I like it when it pours
Because the sound
Drowns out their screams,
Helps with the voices
In their heads,
And I can sit back,
Read on my lunch break
Without the moans of
Hungry spirits
Creeping through the
Cracks in my floor

I like it when it storms
Because the lights go out
And I can pretend I don't
See them fighting,
Don't hear them begging
As the crazies break out
Of their rooms and murder
Their neighbors while they sleep
I pretend I'm not there,

Because when it showers
I go off duty and
Let the asylum drown

Nurse in Ward # 2

I miss them like they were my own
Yet in a way I suppose they were:
Blind, deaf, mute, some of them lame
All of them crazy,
They were my children

Even if they weren't all born
In the asylum, there was no mistaking
That it was all of their homes:
A safe haven that betrayed them in the end
That fooled them into innocence
While it hid behind a soiled cloak

I didn't know what the others had been doing
How they'd been feeding them lies,
Filling their cups full of poison
And their mouths full of their cocks,
I didn't know they were being raped
Being tricked into favors to gain
A few minutes of happiness
Only to be butchered like cattle
And used in experiments

I miss them like they were my own,
But there's a new batch of them here:
Blind, deaf, mute, some of them lame
All of them crazy,
But they are *not* my children
And I do not feel guilty

On My Terms

He stared at me
Eyes ablaze with
Self hatred and regret
As he stood on a patch
Of dead grass and
Crumbled leaves

"Just get the fuck away from me."

A teardrop
Rolled down his cheek,
As he pushed me away
Bruising the only jagged piece
Of heart I had left

"I'm serious."

I stood there in my
Black t-shirt and favorite
Ripped jeans,
Cracking my knuckles
And sliding my hands
Down my side
In that nervous way
I used to get when
I got confused

"You really want me to go?" I said.

He turned,
Started to walk away
Like I never meant

Anything to him,
But the bullet lodged in
His back stopped him
Dead in his tracks
As blood started
To trickle down
The shirt I bought him
Last Christmas

And then I shot him
Six more times-
One for each year
That I wasted my
Life on him

"My pleasure."

Patient Blind

Look at me.
Yes, I can see you
Even if my eyes
Are dead—
I can sense you
Approaching,
Coming closer
With your 20/20,
Your prefect
Crystal blues
Against my pale
Weary orbs
But don't be fooled
By the wisps
Of gray that float
Over them,
That's just my
Soul taking watch
Creeping on the
Forefront of the
Battlefield
As I seek out
Another pair to
Use instead of
My own

Patient Deaf

Silence screams like a banshee
In the night; a woman scorned
That calls me through
Blacked out windows,
Summoning me with
Bleached fangs
And twisted tongues,
A mane of hair covered
In Hell's serpents

The demon tries to suffocate me
Lips moving fast in backwards shrieks
They dig in my ears like razor blades
Draining my blood
In rivers of red
As the pounding
On my ear drum picks up tempo—
Bangs a little louder

Make it stop!
I can't take the noise—
The muted mumbles,
The voiceless yelps—
They're too loud in
Silent foreplay,
Her mouth an oral fixation
Her breath an erotic summons
To the blackness
Her words promise

I'm drowning in unspoken
Soliloquies, pitted against a corner,

Crashing in still reverberation
From voices that echo
Throughout these walls—
My body shakes
Stabbed by the metal slabs of clamor
So loud
So violently earsplitting
That the people around me
Must wonder what evil I hear

Patient Green

The doctor pronounced
Clara green with envy,
Not thinking she wouldn't
Sleep at night for fear that her
Perfect skin would tarnish
Due to her jealous rage
Over her sister's new beau

Clara couldn't deny it,
And in her mind it happened,
Happened like the perfect
Fairy tale ending,
So when the two of them
Visited the ward,
Clara was all too eager
To tell her sister how they fucked
While she was in the restroom
How he laid her down on the bed,
Pumped her full of pleasure
And put on a clean face
By the time she returned

Her sister up and left,
And Clara couldn't stop laughing
Couldn't stop looking
At the face she had painted
The perfect shade of green
As the area in between her legs
Grew moist from the thought
Of her lie

Patient Limb

When I was at home,
I would bend my leg at the knee
And fantasize what it would
Be like to cut it off,
To saw through the meaty fillet
Like a Thanksgiving turkey
And rip it apart like a wishbone,
Waving the stump in the air
For good luck

It used to be enough
To pretend it wasn't there
Like it was some phantom limb
That haunted my skeleton
With an extra appendage
But now I find myself drawing
Lines around my thighs
And checking the blades on the
Chainsaw in the garage
In case my curiosity
For normalcy wins
At the end of the evening

Truth be told,
I didn't think I would do it,
Didn't think that I could,
But when I couldn't shake the weight,
The dead load that hung
Heavy off my torso like a
Pile of wet clothes,
I plugged in the kitchen knife,
The one for the big bird,

And sawed away at that bastard
Until I was free of his presence

By the time the paramedics found me
Bathed in blood on my kitchen floor,
Barely conscious
With a leg in one hand,
A knife in the other
I couldn't help but smile on the
Hospital gurney
Until I realized how heavy,
How utterly disgusting
The remaining leg
Sticking out of the bed sheets
Was as it looked at me

Patient Mute

They sewed up my mouth,
Sealed my lips together
In black fabric,
Threaded them with the steady ease
Of a tailor's hand,
A surgeon's hand,
One whose field of practice
Prevented tongues from spilling
Lies like blood.

They took my voice,
Snuffed it out in a sea of
Medicine—of poison—and
When I couldn't tell them to stop,
They laughed—
Laughed as they butchered
My throat, ripped out my music box
And severed the chords.

In a life of silence I lay awake,
Bathed in a slow decay of
Deafening stillness as I'm
Strangled by the words that
Were left unspoken,
By the screams that were
Never even formed

Penetration

When you told me I could fuck you,
I bet you weren't expecting
The knives, the long silver cocks
That I shoved up inside of you
Like metal dildos from an iron maiden
Kissed with blood

I tried not to use them,
But they've become another
Appendage of mine, sticking
Out of me like sharpened, silver limbs
That help me get off when I
Touch you down there

I didn't appreciate you dying though
It rather hurt my ego when you
Closed your eyes to pain, slept eternally
In a world where I couldn't get to you
And without the fear in your eyes,
The blood that ran down your thighs
Didn't do it for me

Pick Up Line

You look like a man
Who knows his way
Around a woman's body

Someone who could
Read me my sins
And make me repent
Force me pay for them
While I'm down
On my knees

The type of person
Who turns pleasure
Into pain
And love
Into filthy, raw lust

Does that sound
Like the kind of man
That you are?

Cause I'm a woman
Who knows her way
Around a man's body

Someone who could
Read you your sins
And make you repent
While you're choked
And gagged on the
White, cotton sheets
Of my hotel room

I'm the type of person
Who knows nothing
Of pleasure,
But all about pain

And you sir,
Well…

You're the kind of man
That knows everything
About satisfaction,
Everything about taking
What you want
When you want it
No matter who
Gets hurt in the end

But this time
You're going to pick
Up the wrong girl
And
When you come up
To my hotel room
You won't feel pleasure
And you won't feel pain

In fact, if I'm correct
In saying this,
I hear that the dead
Don't feel much of anything
At all

Repetition

I'm running nowhere,
With no destination
No safe house in sight
Just running
Just trying to get away
To escape the labyrinth
That has become my mind
The puzzle that traps me
Locks me in hell
In a prison I can't solve
My way out of

I see clouds of gray
Portals that shine
As if they were constructed
By fallen stars,
Dimensions that open
Only to close when the
Nightmares have crawled
Out and sniffed my scent,
Got the taste of my blood
On their tongues

I weave in and out of dreams
Like an amputated seamstress
Hobbling through the pain,
Limping in the tragedy
But I can hear them behind me,
Grunting as they get closer
Breathing heavy as they
Choke on my fear
Yet I don't wake up

When they kill me,
I just keep starting over,
Rewinding back to the
Beginning of the maze
Waiting to see what hand
Fate has dealt me,
Curious as to how
I'll die all over again

Resilient

The first time I died
It was quick and
Sharp as a bolt of lightning
But not very memorable;
I didn't even get a chance
To scream bloody murder

Gunshot to the head.

The second time I died
It was strung out and
Slow as a sloth on a
Hot summer day
But not much
Worth talking about;
I couldn't even cry
Because I was dehydrated

Left to die in the streets.

The third time I died
It was at my hand,
Perfectly paced and
Almost done according
To plan except I couldn't
Write my suicide note
Because I kept vomiting
Up the poison.

Drank the pesticide.

The fourth time I died

I prayed I wouldn't come back
But like the bad luck charm
I etched around my wrist,
There I stood,
Bound to repeat the cycle
Over and over again

Stuck in Purgatory.

Shower Scene

Water doesn't baptize me—
There's nothing cleansing
About the wet rape in the
Second stall,
Nothing holy about the
Shame that washes
Off my body like
Second-hand dirt

Give me fire any day—
An element that knows
What it is to truly burn,
To take the past
And turn it to ash,
To drag my demons
By the hair
Listening as they scream

Shut In

The fire lulls me to sleep,
Dances like a red goddess
Amongst the coals
While the ashes burn my eyes—
I blink away tears

A tattered blanket covers me,
Sheer and moth-eaten,
I've spent days in this hole,
Festering in ice and filth—
I am no longer warm

The stone walls give off a draft
But the solitude of my space
Rings happily in my ears,
A familiar tune of loneliness—
I sit pent up in my cottage

But the fire starts to fade
My eyes lose their focus,
Blurred visions, shaken images
Reality starts to return—
I pray for the illusion to stay

Signature

I picked you from the phone book
I liked the way your name sounded
It rolled off my lips
And made me hard
Because it sounded exotic

People stared at me on the bus
I guess they frown
When you masturbate in public
But I couldn't get your name
Out of my head
So I got off the bus
And finished on the sidewalk
Near the lamppost in front of your house

I sat on your doorstep
But didn't ring your doorbell
I wanted to see if you could feel me there
Waiting to see you
To see the face that fits the name
But you never came out
So I took out my knife
And carved my name
On one of your cement steps
Just in case my name
Had the same effect on you

Sloth

The sheets were his clothing
The pillows his crown,
Yet Jameson was happy
Because he never moved
To experience anything other
Than the indolent bliss he was used to

For him, life had finally became simple
It unwound itself from
The horrors and difficulties he
Used to face:
Unemployment
Divorce
Child Support
His sloth became his savior,
The forgiving parent that
Wrapped his child in his arms,
Telling him everything was alright,
But it was his idle mind
That devoured the sin in gulps
Of passivity and unconscious indulgence,
Capturing him in his bed,
But not holding him prisoner

He grew to like the quiet:
The dull ease of white noise
And slow death,
The essence of never being tired
With sleep only a closed eyelid away
And thus, stationary he remained,
Bedridden and swaddled in sweat
Festering in his own lethargy

Like a half-dead slug begging for salt
Because for Jameson,
It was easier not to move,
Than to take a chance
And start living again

Solitary

Alone,
Trapped in darkness
She buries herself
In black,
Pulls the sheets
Over her face
Like the lid to her coffin
No noise
Just the reverberations
Of silent static
To will her into sleep
So she can wake up
In order to live
Her single-serving life
Locked away
In confinement

Stalker

Backwards
Frontwards
Sideways
Upside-down
Right-side up
To my left
To my right
At the bus-stop
Waiting outside work
Across the street
In the car behind me
Outside my window
On the phone
In my answering machine
Tucked into my mailbox
In line at the store
Six rows behind me at the game
Next to me at the concert
Following me home
Watching me sleep
Waiting for tomorrow

Stockholm

My body aches
From where you cut me—
A jagged reminder
Of a haunted past,
A sharpened memento
Of a hostage romance

Storm

Lightning courses through my brain
Subtle shocks that shake me
Followed by a bellowing thunder
In the depths of my cortex

I feel the electricity,
My temples the socket
As they plug the silver wires
Into my head, into my flesh
The sparks light up my eyes
Dance in the channels
Of my transmitters,
Run rapid in the crevasses
They bury themselves into
Like snakes in my skull

My body goes as rigid
As the gurney I lay on,
Toes curled and cracked
My tongue bleeding and spiked
From where my incisors
Bit through it
I'm alive on the outside
But dead inside,
Wandering in a dense fog
That clouds my vision
Until the next storm strikes

Straight Jacket

Claustrophobia sets in
I twist and turn
Jingling the locks
That are fastened
Around my hands
And feet
But I go nowhere
That I haven't
Already been
In my head

You see,
The men in white,
Don't let me go
Anywhere and keep
Me folded up like
Some pretzel in an oven
All because I tried to
Keep myself clean

I mean
How else was
I supposed to get them—
The creepy crawlies
That withered underneath my flesh,
Burrowed into my scalp,
Breeding incessantly
While I tried to scratch off my skin

But it didn't work,
They were feeding off me—
Gnawing on my bones,

Flossing with my veins,
You see, I had no choice!
I had to do it—these parasites
Caused disease, infection and
I could feel it spreading within me
As they multiplied within my flesh

So I went into the kitchen,
Tiptoeing slowly,
Quietly, carefully,
Not wanting them to hear me
As I grabbed the kitchen knife

I broke open my skin
But they must have hid
Because nothing was there,
No scurrying black dots,
No eight-legged freaks,
So I dug in deeper
Dug until my arm went numb
I would find them,
Oh yes I would
But those bastards were probably
Eating me from the inside now
Tying my veins in knots
Slurping up my blood
Gorging themselves on my cells

The paramedics didn't believe me
The doctors yelled at me
No one would listen
They said I tried to kill myself
But I was exterminating
It was they who amputated my arm
Not me

But in the end—
Let me tell you something
I won, and I did so
In my clean, pressed white shirt,
With one arm tied
Singlehandedly behind my back

Stranger

I pray to the moon
But she does not listen
To my prayers
Instead she mocks me
Like an abusive mother
Drowning me in absence
As I flirt with lightening,
Sleep with thunder

I stay up at night looking for her
Like a lost child
In a crowd of strangers,
Searching the skies for a sign,
A signal that she's been watching
Even though I know
She doesn't care

Abandoned at birth,
I walk among the forgotten
Damned with a curse
I cannot understand
And a mother who's too far away,
Too stubborn to teach me
How to grow up
And be a member of her pack

Tea Party

Cadence likes her tea
She throws parties every afternoon
Inviting her imaginary friends
Serving up fake
Cucumber sandwiches
In the corner of her room

A 42-year-old woman,
She cradles a stuffed rabbit
In her arms,
Holding it tight to her chest
As if it would crumble
Should she let it go

The doctors study her
Like a child holding
A magnifying glass
Over an ant hill on a
Warm, sunny day—
Waiting for her to break
So they can rush in
With their tools,
Poke and prod her
Like roadkill on the side
Of the street

Cadence offers them a cup
Comes up to the door
With a smile on her face,
A grin that says
They'll never get their chance,
That madness can't be cured,

Yet ever the gracious hostess
She returns to her guests
To tend to their needs

Tell Me I'm Yours

I spit in his mouth.
Tell me I'm yours.
He declines.

The blade glides across his neck,
My lips hungry for his blood
Insatiable thirst
Exceptional lust
A dead man's heart beats in my hand

I pull on his lips.
Tell me I'm yours.
He declines.

The blade trickles down his chest
Slicing his pores
Erotic arousal
Chilling orgasm
His cold eyes staring into mine

I grab his throat.
Tell me I'm yours.
He declines.

The blade slices his abdomen
I put my hand in the warmth
Shivering fright
Petrified tension
His life leaving his body on my watch.

I suck his tongue.
Tell me I'm yours.

He declines.

But in death, he accepts.

That Room

The walls
They look like big marshmallows
Padded and cushioned
From top to bottom
So I don't hurt myself
When I walk into them,
Or run

The Artist

He looked at it with
Hollow eyes,
Blackened from years
Of stone stares
As the creases near his
Mouth began to
Quiver

He waved the blade,
Reflecting light
Off its silver tip
And hacked off
The pieces he didn't like—
The ones that haunted
Him like severed limbs
Amputated in the
Back of his mind,
Poking at his
Subconscious
With phantom
Boughs

He chopped them up,
Slashed and scattered
The leftover
Fruits of his labor,
And lay down in their
Remains
Consuming them like a
Cat eats the afterbirth
Of its young,
Devouring his failure

Like a man twice
Starved for his
Art

The Cheater

You want my bloody kiss
Stop denying it
Accept the crimson red
Smear it all over your face
Lean into it
Suck on my lip
And savor the bitterness
Of your lover's death

You see,
I loved her gently
Moved inside her easy
Made love to her
With a chainsaw
And watched the life
Leave her eyes
Don't worry though,
She suffered.

The Color White

White reminds me of bone,
Of marrow being sucked out of me
On a frozen, snow-covered plate
While bleach is poured down my throat
To cleanse me, and sterilize my blood

I don't see clean,
I see covered up filth
Black lights on white sheets
Violation and screaming impurities
Crystal tears in a sea of what used
To be abstinence

White reminds me of teeth,
Of his crooked smile and
Elongated canines; the absence
Of his reflection in my bedroom mirror and
The icy touch of his skin against my cheek

White is supposed to be comforting
But the gloved hands of the people
Sticking tubes down my throat
Don't make me feel that way;
A sense of calm doesn't rush over me
When I see their white jackets rushing
At me like I'm a closet case who's
Faking an attack

White is supposed to be blissful
But it hurts my eyes
And I'm sick of hurting
And I'm tired of this color

Being everywhere I go
In this damn hospital
Because every time I see it,
I feel the walls close in a little more
I feel his blank eyes stare straight through me
Because first and foremost,
White reminds me of blood
And the two holes punched
In the side of my neck

The Conductor

I sit there patiently
As droplets of water
Slide down my cheek
While the sponge in
My hat is compressed
From the weight on my
Overused skull cap

They've strapped me in
Like they think I'm
Going to run away
But I wouldn't trade
Their shock for all
The conductors
And outlets in the prison

My eyes followed the
Cords as they snaked
Up to the metal lever
Watching with excitement
As the County Warden
Pulled down the switch
Hungry for the sweat
Mixed water glistening
Against my temples

I wiggled my fingers,
Twitched them back to life
As white-hot jolts shot
Out of my body like a
Hail storm at dawn

One by one they fell
The stench of rotting flesh
Creeping through the room
As their pale skin turned black
And flaked off like snow

Damn fools thought
They could electrocute me,
Take me out at my own game
But they didn't know
That I have a habit of
Sparking on my own

The Crematorium

The smell of leather excites me
Reminds me of the belt you tied me up with
But now it's you on the cold, metal slab
Entering the fire through the open window

The soles of your feet caught first
Your screams filled the soundproof room
As you pissed yourself from the pain,
An acrid, bitter smell lingering in the air

Your begging made me horny
As your sweat began to sour
And your black skin peeled off
Revealing a juicy, medium rare pink center
I couldn't help but salivate

The fire ravaged your thighs
Eating away at you hungrily
And I'll admit,
I love the smell of charred flesh,
And watching your manhood burn
Made me wet

The Necklace

The rope burned my hands,
My hair got caught in the knot,
I twisted it.

I wore my best dress,
My most fashionable shoes
Skinny stilettos that looked like daggers.

I put on my choker,
(It was always my favorite necklace)
I stepped off the stool,
And danced in the air.

Think of Me

Your shadow dances on the shower wall
Seducing me with its rhythmic silhouette
As I see you wash yourself
From head to toe,
Your hands and fingers lingering
On your throbbing cock,
As you stoke it,
With droplets of burning water
Penetrating through your skin

I'm watching you
From the crack in the door
Feeling the steam collide with my face
Your scent lingering in the air
Flooding my nostrils
My own aphrodisiac

So keep playing.

Lather yourself up, baby
Try and cover your skin from my preying eyes
Because I'm already taking off my shirt
Nipples erect, with moistness between my legs
And my pussy is calling your name
But then again,
So is my knife

Tell me.

Did you think of me when you fucked her?
Drilled her from behind
Spraying your juice on our shower curtain

Leaving a permanent stain
A constant reminder
Of your adulterous behavior

Did you think of me when you dried her off?
Licking her navel
Toweling her off with my cotton blanket
Trying to wipe away your mark
When it was already burned into her flesh?

No?

Well I thought of you when I fucked her
When I pushed her silky hair away from her face
And kissed her eyelashes,
While I slit her throat
And licked the blood off her breasts

And I'll think of her when I fuck you
My tongue dancing around your dick
Playfully swallowing your balls in my mouth
Before I castrate you
And leave you to die
With nothing but me on your mind

Turn Off the Nightmares

by

Michael Arnzen and Stephanie Wytovich

erase my trauma, my fears
lobotomize me
turn off the nightmares

turn off the nightmares
throw the electrical switch
wired to my skull cap

wired to my skull cap
the one that makes my mouth bleed
makes my eyes fade black

my eyes fade to black—
giving this snuff film
an appropriate ending

Unknown

He may not
Know my name
But he knows
Who I am,
What I am,
But never where

Unravel

Stitched from the neck down,
I snip the thread
Watch myself unravel
Loosening the bound ribbon
That was sewn into my skin
Like a delicate corset
Laying across my back

A fabric shell converts to
A portrait of unwinding
Veins and arteries
Etched in a raspberry wine
Flowing down in knotted proportions
While ripping capillaries
Dance the red cell tango
Down my thighs,
Dipping their partners —
Moving faster to the rhythm
Of the orchestrated heart beat

I'm dressed in this ivory gown
My bones glistening in the dim light
As they shed their skin,
Exhuming framework that is
Stronger than any piece of art;
With black gaping holes for eye sockets
And toothy pearl cubes for a smile
That would give the Mona Lisa
A run for her money

My simple composition
Hypnotizes your eyes to count

Down to my last vertebrae,
Weaving in and out of the layered blocks
Snapped together at the ends
Like buttons on a winter jacket,
Carefully constructing an outline—
The bones progressively stronger
As your eyes move down my body,
Lost in the transition of my
Chameleon-like state,
As I step out of my skin
And take the first step
Of my *inhuman* life
So I can blend in with the dead
Since no one is longer alive

Vagina Dentata

What do you tell a girl
When you don't want
To have sex with her,
When you can't
Have sex with her,
Because you're afraid
Of her lady parts,
Of what's hiding
Underneath her pants

What do you do
When she's in front of you
Taking off her thong,
Spinning it around
On her finger
And it's all you can do
Not to run away
From fear of being
Castrated?
Of having your dick
Ripped off
From her sharply
Toothed genitals?

What do you do
When she asks you
What's wrong,
Why you won't
Touch her
And keep backing away,
And it's all you can do
Not to look the monster

In the eye
And tempt it
Out of its cave?

Vampire

Rumors spread

"They call him the vampire—
Say he'll drink your blood
Or make you bleed
In order to get his fix"

"I heard he
He won't eat,
Doesn't drink anything
They bring him
So they had to hook him
Up to an IV to sustain him"

Lies begin to swell

"Janice told me he
Killed his wife when
His was son was born"

"Yeah, he licked all
The blood in between
Her legs before taking
Her to the hospital—
By then she was
Already dead."

The web continues to grow

"They say he sleeps all day,
Doesn't start moving
Around till night falls,

And all he does is scream
For her"

"Maybe he didn't do it—
The man could be innocent
Like most of us are,
Maybe they just made a mistake"

The air grows cold.

"Or maybe they didn't."

Villain

It may rain when you cry
But people die when I'm mad—
Who has the better superpower?

Voices

Nothing likes to talk to me
It beckons me with silent
Conversation
Tempting me with unspoken
Promises like
    Hushed assurances
Through the broken walls of
Absence built around my head

Like a cricket in my brain
It chirps its summer song
Repeatedly
Nagging at me with needles
Digging further
    Piercing deeper
Into crevices that wind
Like rivers through my brain

The voices fill the contours
Drowning my cranium helmet
Overflowing
Fragmented fissures
    Cracked crannies
Settling into my control system
Telling me what to do
And when to do it

Word Vomit

I swallowed your opinion
But felt it lodge itself
In the back of my throat
Next to the other insults
That I tried to digest
When you laughed
At me on the bus
That morning,
Passing out judgments
As fast as a free cup
Of coffee on Thursdays,
Spitting them out carefree
Like you knew me,
Like we were friends

But we weren't,
And you were a stranger.
You had no idea of the
Night I just had,
Where I drowned my regrets
On the streets,
Alone
Hands glued to a paper bag
Eyes lost somewhere
In the back of my head

You don't know me,
You never will
And as I sat there,
I tried to bite my tongue,
Tried to think of
Anything else
Other than your head

Spiked on a stick,
But I could feel the words
Climbing up my throat,
Spelling out curses as they
Crawled around in
My esophagus
Like spiders spinning
Webs of witty comebacks
And clever clichés

I heard my stomach rumble,
Knew I couldn't keep it down,
Like a egg sac imbedded on my tongue,
Their silky letters made
Me gag
As they scattered around
In my mouth,
And before I could make
My clever retort
I puked up my alphabet soup
Right in your face

Acknowledgements:

For years I've worked within the realms of madness, collecting patients and administering treatments, when and regardless of whether, they were needed. But before I started the Madhouse, a slew of mentors, family, and friends nudged me along the way to accepting the dark muse that plagued me, Hysteria.

I've had the pleasure of working with Michael A. Arnzen, my mentor and friend, since 2007. He's been my greatest influence and a constant source of encouragement, support, and drive. He's taught me not to be afraid to go where my writing takes me, but also not to take myself too seriously, and remember to have fun. I can't thank you enough for everything you've done for me, Mike. It means the world to me.

I also want to thank Lawrence C. Connolly for all of his help and support with this project. Without you, I don't know that I would have had the courage to put *Hysteria* together and start sending her out into the world. Chris Shearer, you've been my backbone through this process and know my madness better than most people. I couldn't ask for a better friend, or critique partner. Thanks for keeping me sane.

Heidi and Jason Miller, I can't thank you enough for everything you've done for me. After this, I owe you both a gallon of Tiger Coffee and a box of gourmet cupcakes. And to my RDSP family, I thank you all for everything. Jen and John, you've been wonderful friends and colleagues and I couldn't be happier working with anyone else.

But most importantly, I want to thank my family.

Mom, thank you for always loving and supporting me no matter how weird or demented my ideas turned out to be. My stories and poems will always be splashed with gore because I know it's your favorite. Dad, thank you for passing down your lyrical and poetic talents to me. I know horror isn't necessarily your favorite, but it means a lot to me that you let me scare you on a regular basis. And Scott. Thank you for being the perfect brainstorming partner, my most honest critic, and the best friend and brother that I could ask for. Without all of you, I never would have had the courage to go after my nightmares and confine them to the page. I love you.

About the Author

Stephanie M. Wytovich is an Alum of Seton Hill University where she was a double major in English Literature and Art History. Wytovich is published in over 40 literary magazines and *Hysteria* is her first collection. She is currently attending graduate school to pursue her MFA in Writing Popular Fiction, and is working on a novel. She is the Poetry Editor for Raw Dog Screaming Press and a book reviewer for S.T. Joshi, Jason V. Brock and William F. Nolan's *Nameless Magazine*. She plans to continue in academia to get her doctorate in Gothic Literature.

CPSIA information can be obtained at www.ICGtesting.com
Printed in the USA
BVOW072016110713

325261BV00001B/14/P